Kids Camp Out

Written by Jill Eggleton

Illustrated by Clive Taylor

Rigby

"We are going
to the beach,"
said Dad.

"Look at the map,"
he said.
"Kids can read."

3

"Go down the road and over the bridge," said the kids.

4

Dad went down the road.

He went over the bridge.

He went into the mud!

"Look at the map,"
said Dad.
"Kids can read."

"Go down the road
and under the trees,"
said the kids.

Dad went down the road.

He went under the trees.

He went into a hole!

"I will look at the map,"
said Dad.

Dad went up the road.

He went over the bridge
and into town.

"This is not the beach!"
said the kids.
"This is a coffee shop!"

"Kids **can** read!"
said Dad.

A Map

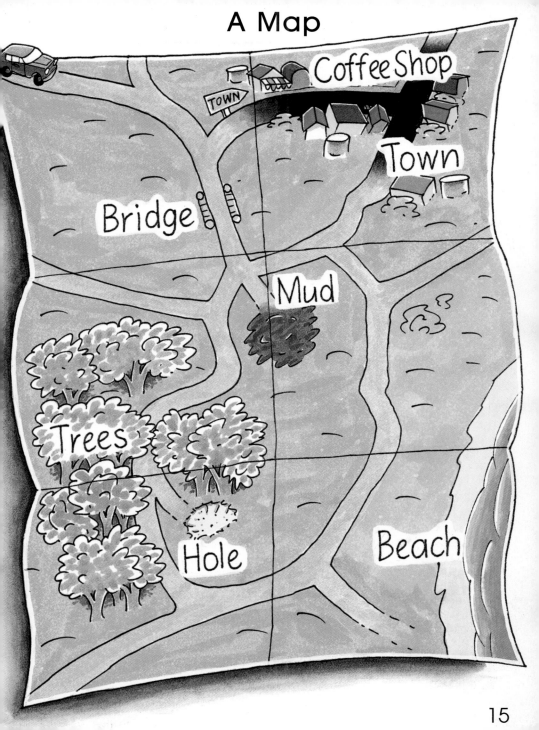

Guide Notes

Title: Kids Can Read
Stage: Early (1) – Red

Genre: Fiction
Approach: Guided Reading
Processes: Thinking Critically, Exploring Language, Processing Information
Written and Visual Focus: Map

THINKING CRITICALLY
(sample questions)
- What do you think this story could be about?
- What do you think the kids are looking at?
- What do you know about a map?
- When would you use a map?
- Why do you think Dad went into the mud?
- How do you think Dad feels about being in a hole?
- What do you think Dad should do?
- Look at page 12. Where do you think Dad could be going?
- Why do you think he is going to a coffee shop?
- How do you think Dad knows the kids can read?

EXPLORING LANGUAGE

Terminology
Title, cover, illustrations, author, illustrator

Vocabulary
Interest words: map, mud
High-frequency words: we, are, to, going, at, the, he, said, can, go, went, I, will, this, is, not, look
Positional words: down, under, over, into, up

Print Conventions
Capital letter for sentence beginnings and name (**D**ad), periods, exclamation marks, quotation marks, commas